THE CALM
AFTER
THE STORM

by Christopher Klausen
illustrated by Roberta Wilson

Harcourt

SCHOOL PUBLISHERS

Printed in China

ISBN 10: 0-15-351528-7
ISBN 13: 978-0-15-351528-6

Ordering Options
ISBN 10: 0-15-351214-8 (Grade 4 Advanced Collection)
ISBN 13: 978-0-15-351214-8 (Grade 4 Advanced Collection)
ISBN 10: 0-15-358118-3 (package of 5)
ISBN 13: 978-0-15-358118-2 (package of 5)

5 6 7 8 9 10 985 12 11 10 09

"Davis, did you take a look at that calf's foot?" my father asked. My father was on top of every little detail, which is probably what made him so successful. The ranch he started, the Big T Ranch, is one of the largest in north Texas. It's called the "Big T" because our last name is Tate.

"I sure did, Pa, and it looks fine," I told him. Most of the time Pa trusted what I said. I'd been born and raised on the ranch, and now, by age twelve, I'd come to learn a lot about cattle and horses.

It was April, the time when the crew prepares for the big cattle drive. That's when a large herd of cattle is moved from the ranch to one of the railroad towns up north to be sold.

Getting the cattle from our ranch near Dallas all the way to Kansas City, Missouri, is no easy task. There aren't any railroads down here, so the cattle have to be walked. Usually, it takes about fifteen people to do the job.

The cattle drive is always in the spring because by that time of the year, plenty of grass has grown, so the cows have food to eat. Pa explained that if the cows look too thin, no one up north will want to buy them. The crew lets the cows do a lot of grazing and eating while they move north. Because of the slow pace, the drive takes weeks or even months.

"Pa, I want to go on the drive this year," I said one day. "For years, I've listened to the crew tell their stories. I know it's a lot of hard work and drudgery, but I think I'm old enough now to handle it."

Pa paused and then peered into my eyes, as if he were looking inside of me to see whether I had what it took to go on a drive. Finally, he said, "Okay, kiddo, but we're going to have to make sure it's all right with your mother."

"Thanks, Pa, I won't let you down," I said, and then I let out a loud whoop.

"Davis, you're going to be a wrangler," Sam told me one day in late April. Sam was my father's trail boss, the fellow who was in charge of leading the whole cattle drive. He was a stern, serious man, but he was hard-working and fair.

I liked the idea of being a wrangler because I was good with horses. The wrangler takes care of the extra horses. There are always extra horses on a drive in case a horse gets sick or needs a rest.

"I told your father I would look after you, but I'm going to be busy out there, so you're going to have to do a lot on your own," Sam explained. "Also, you have to do what the others tell you."

"You won't have to worry about me, Sam," I said.

Early on a Saturday morning at the start of May, it was time to hit the trail. "You stay safe and listen to Sam," Momma told me, and then she gave me a hug and a kiss.

"I'll be fine, Momma," I said and hugged her back. My father and I shook hands, and I hopped up on Dart, my horse.

I rode over to Carlo, the other wrangler, and together we got the extra horses rounded up and walked them up behind the chuck wagon. The chuck wagon carries all the food and blankets for the drive. It is always at the very front of the line so that the food doesn't get dusty. The wranglers and extra horses are next in line, followed by the cattle and the crew who guide them.

Off we went, up the Shawnee Trail toward Kansas City, with almost three thousand head of cattle. The first day of the drive wasn't too bad. As we rode, I kept an eye on the horses and looked at the scenery.

"Hey!" yelled Carlo, startling me. "Get that horse!" I looked and saw that an older horse behind me had broken free from the pack. I quickly chased it down and returned it. Carlo looked over at me skeptically, as if I didn't know what I was doing.

"That wasn't fast enough—the horse would have been lost if I hadn't told you," he sputtered. For the rest of the day, Carlo didn't speak to me.

That night, we set up camp, ate, sat by the smoldering fire, and prepared our bedrolls. After I pulled my boots off and was about to get under my covers, Carlo said, "You *sure* you want to get in there?" He pointed at my blanket, and I saw a large scorpion crawling across it. I smashed it with my boot and thanked Carlo for helping me avert a disaster.

"*Thank you, Carlo*? You think saying *thank you* is going to help you on this drive? You better start using your head," he scoffed.

I went to bed feeling angry with Carlo for yelling at me and angry with myself for not remembering to look out for scorpions. "Tomorrow I'll alter my behavior," I thought, as I faded off to sleep.

At sunrise, I got dressed and started to gather up my things. A moment later Carlo came up from behind me. "Where's my water sack, kid?" he yelled furiously.

"I don't know where it is, Carlo," I said, pulling away from him.

"Where did you hide it—in your pack? On your horse?" he yelled. Just then, Sam walked over carrying a water sack.

"This was by the wagon, Carlo," he said, holding it up. Carlo took it without saying a word. Then Sam pulled me to the side and said, "I think you've spent enough time with Carlo, so today I want you to ride drag."

Riding drag was about the worst job a cattle driver could have. The drag riders stayed at the back of the herd to make sure none of the cows fell too far behind or got lost.

The very worst part of riding drag was the dust. When thousands of cows walk a dusty trail in front of you, they kick up loads of dust, and the riders in the rear get it all in their faces.

"Cover your mouth with a handkerchief," said Mack, the other drag rider. I did so, and it helped, but dust still got into my eyes and slowed me down. I much preferred being a wrangler up front, but at least back here I was far away from Carlo.

For days we rode through rain, wind, and dust storms, chased after loose cows, and kept an eye out for treacherous wolves. Overall it was pretty discouraging. I thought we would never get where we were going.

One day, late in the afternoon, the sky quickly grew dark. Then, in what seemed like just a moment, a ferocious storm was upon us. We saw lightning hit the ground and heard a loud crash of thunder.

One of the cows was startled by the thunder and bolted off the trail. The rest of the cows followed, too, and all of a sudden there was a stampede! Three thousand frightened cattle were charging away at full speed. Sam galloped after the lead cow on his horse, while the other cowboys rode as fast as they could to try to slow down the stampeding cows.

Suddenly, through the rain, I saw Carlo riding alongside a small group of stampeding cows, trying to slow them down. When he bent over to throw his rope, he accidentally slid out of his saddle and plunged to the ground. Another group of stampeding cows was coming his way.

Without even thinking, I turned Dart to the left and sped toward Carlo. He had gotten back on his feet, but his horse was long gone. I pushed Dart harder to increase my speed and yelled, "CARLO!" I raced toward him, slowed down a little, and then extended my arm. Carlo grabbed my arm and saddle, and he pulled himself up on my horse just as the cows blasted past us. It was a close call, but we both survived.

That night in camp, the storm and stampede had ended, and the cows were back under control. All was calm. Carlo came up to me. "Thank you," he said.

"*Thank you*, Carlo? You think saying *thank you* is going to help you on this drive?" I asked playfully. He remembered that he had said that to me, and then he looked at me with a sheepish smile.

"Sorry I was so tough on you, kid," he said. "Hey, how about you being a wrangler with me again? I'll talk to Sam."

"Absolutely," I said, happy to get out of the dust. After the scorpion, the storm, and the stampede, I knew I could handle anything—even Carlo.

Think Critically

1. Why does Sam change Davis's job?

2. What problem did Davis face when he was the drag rider?

3. How do you think Davis and Carlo would get along if this story continued? Why?

4. Using context clues, explain what *drudgery* means on page 5.

5. How did you feel when Davis saved Carlo?

 Science

Make a Poster In this story there is a big thunderstorm. Find out some facts about thunderstorms and how they form. Then make a poster of thunderstorm facts.

School-Home Connection Share the story with family members. Include the part about there being 3,000 cows on the drive. Take turns comparing 3,000 cows to other things to get an idea of how many cows that is. For example, if each cow were a day, the days would add up to more than eight years.